Copyright © Lovers Lane Investments. All Rights Reserved.

TELE

DISTANT OR FAR

My **tele**scope can look at the stars in the distance.

PHON

SOUND

I can talk to my grandma on my telephone.

GRAPH/GRAM

WRITE OR DRAW

Can I have your autograph?

AUTO
SELF

I think we are flying on autopilot!

PHOTO

LIGHT

The photograph captures the light perfectly.

SCOPE

TO WATCH OR SEE

Beautiful colors can be seen through a fun toy called a kaleidoscope.

MICRO

SMALL OR MINUTE

We can see tiny objects under a microscope.

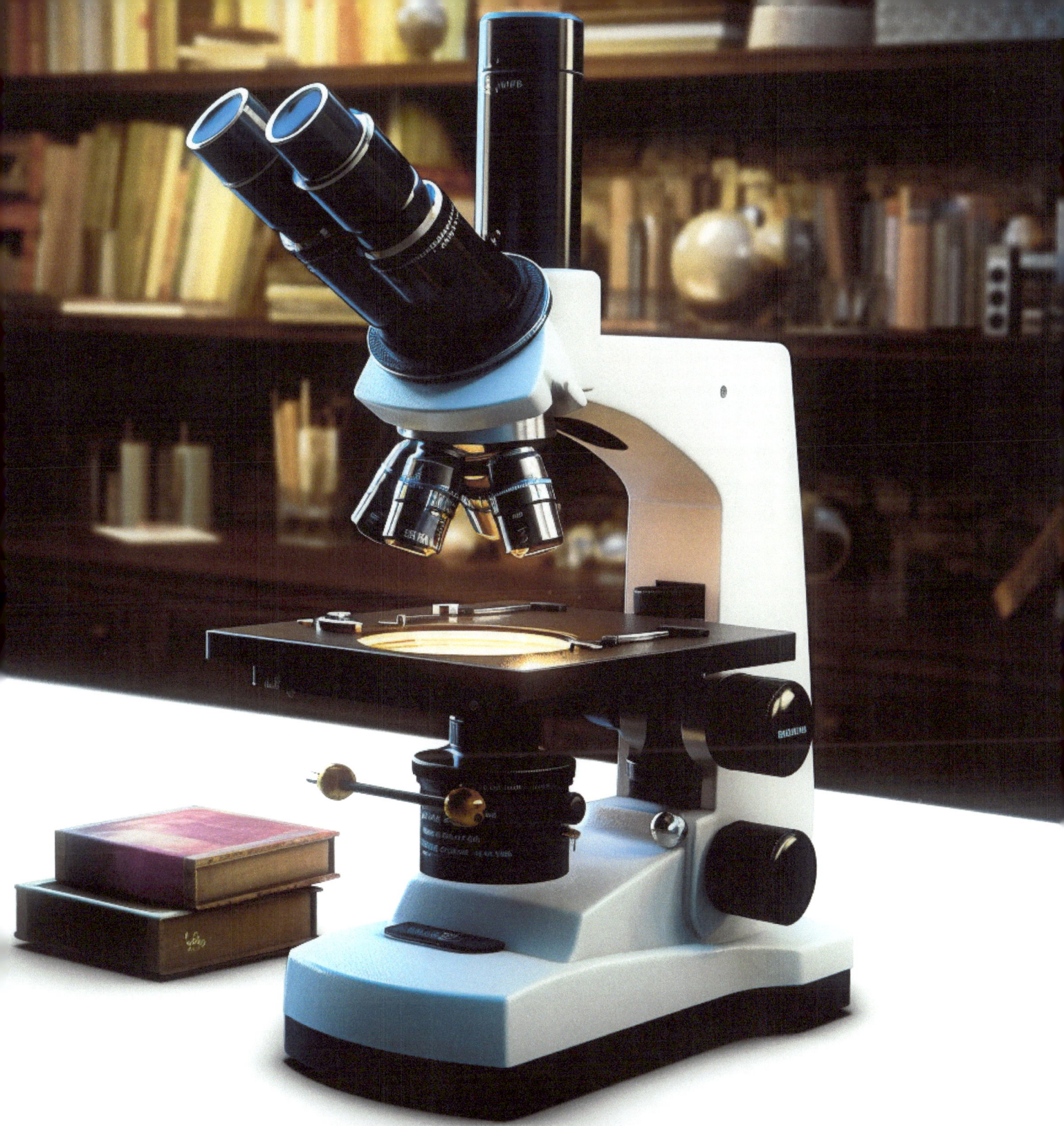

(O)LOGY
THE SCIENCE OR STUDY OF

Bio**logy** is the study of living things.

HYDR(O)
WATER

The firefighters used water out of the **hydr**ant to put out the fire.

BIBLIO
BOOK

A **biblio**graphy is a list of books and articles that an author used to write their report.

BIO

LIFE

A **bio**nic limb can replace your arm.

PHOBIA

IRRATIONAL FEAR OR HATRED OF

If you have arachno*phobia*, you probably do not like these little guys.

THERMO

HEAT OR HOT

My thermos is perfect for keeping my cocoa hot.

METER/METR

MEASURE

I can measure the outside peri*meter* of the soccer field.

GEO

EARTH

A **geo**logist studies rocks on Earth.

CYCLE

WHEEL, CIRCLE, OR RING

A bicycle has only two wheels.

CHRON(O)
TIME

The soldiers were synchron**ized in their routine.**

PSYCH

MIND OR SOUL

You must be psychic because you read my mind!

SPHERE

BALL

Our atmosphere is the layer of gases around the Earth.

PATH

FEELING, SUFFERING, OR DISEASE

Show some sym**path**y when your friends are sad.

1. **tele** - telescope, telegram, telepathic, telepathy, television, telephone
2. **phon** - megaphone, microphone, phoneme, phonics, homophone, symphony
3. **graph/gram** - autograph, digraph, telegraph, graphic, grapheme, polygraph
4. **auto** - autopilot, automatic, automaticity, autonomy, automobile, autoimmune
5. **photo** - photography, photon, photosynthesis, photographic, photographer
6. **scope** - telescope, horoscope, microscope, stethoscope, spectroscope
7. **micro** - microscopic, microbiology, micron, microwave, microbial, microbe
8. **(o)logy** - biology, reflexology, psychology, anthropology, cosmetology, zoology
9. **hydr(o)** - hydrant, hydration, hydrogen, hydraulics, hydrotherapy, hydroplane
10. **biblio** - bibliography, bibliographer, bibliographies, Bible
11. **bio** - bionic, biology, biome, biosphere, biography, biopsy, symbiosis, antibiotic
12. **phobia** - claustrophobia, acrophobia, hydrophobia, xenophobia, phobias
13. **thermo** - thermos, hypothermia, thermal, geothermic, thermostat, thermoplastic
14. **meter/metr** - perimeter, centimeter, odometer, kilometer, parameter, barometer
15. **geo** - geologist, geographic, geothermal, geopolitics, geometry
16. **cycle** - bicycle, recycle, unicycle, tricycle, cyclone, cyclist, motorcycle, cyclops
17. **chron(o)** - synchronized, chronological, chronology, chronic, chronicle, synchronous
18. **psych** - psychic, psychology, psychologist, psychiatric, psychotic, psyche
19. **sphere** - atmosphere, hemisphere, stratosphere, troposphere, biosphere
20. **path** - sympathy, pathology, empathetic, empathy, sympathetic, antipathetic